An I Can Read Book®

THE LITTLE BEAR TREASURY

by

ELSE HOLMELUND MINARIK

pictures by MAURICE SENDAK

HarperCollinsPublishers

THE LITTLE BEAR TREASURY

For information address HarperCollins Children's Books, a division of HarperCollins Publishers, 10 East 53rd Street, New York, NY 10022.

Reprinted by permission of HarperCollins Publishers.

ISBN 0-06-027398-4

CONTENTS

An I Can Read Book®

LITTLE BEAR

by

ELSE HOLMELUND MINARIK

pictures by MAURICE SENDAK

HarperTrophy®
A Division of HarperCollins*Publishers*

TO BROOKE ELLEN AND WALLY

CONTENTS

LITTLE BEAR

WHAT WILL LITTLE BEAR WEAR?

It is cold.

See the snow.

See the snow come down.

Little Bear said, "Mother Bear,

I am cold.

See the snow.

I want something to put on."

So Mother Bear made something
for Little Bear.
"See, Little Bear," she said,
"I have something for my little bear.
Here it is.

"Put it on your head."

"Oh," said Little Bear,

"it is a hat.

Hurray! Now I will not be cold."

Little Bear went out to play.

Here is Little Bear.

"Oh," said Mother Bear,

"do you want something?"

"I am cold," said Little Bear.

"I want something to put on."

So Mother Bear made something

for Little Bear.

"See, Little Bear," she said,
"I have something,
something for my little bear.
Put it on."
"Oh," said Little Bear,
"it is a coat.
Hurray! Now I will not be cold."
Little Bear went out to play.

Here is Little Bear again.

"Oh," said Mother Bear,

"do you want something?"

"I am cold," said Little Bear.

"I want something to put on."

So Mother Bear made something again for Little Bear.
"See, Little Bear," she said,
"here is something,
something for my little bear.
Now you cannot be cold.
Put it on."

"Oh," said Little Bear,
"snow pants. Hurray!
Now I will not be cold."
Little Bear went out to play.

Here is Little Bear again.

"Oh," said Mother Bear,

"what can you want now?"

"I am cold," said Little Bear.

"I want something to put on."

"My little bear," said Mother Bear,

"you have a hat,

you have a coat,

you have snow pants.

Do you want a fur coat, too?"

"Yes," said Little Bear.
"I want a fur coat, too."

Mother Bear took the hat, the coat,
and the snow pants.
"See," said Mother Bear,
"there is the fur coat."

"Hurray!" said Little Bear.
"Here is my fur coat.
Now I will not be cold."

And he was not cold.

What do you think of that?

BIRTHDAY SOUP

"Mother Bear,

Mother Bear,

Where are you?" calls Little Bear.

"Oh, dear, Mother Bear is not here,

and today is my birthday.

"I think my friends will come,
but I do not see a birthday cake.
My goodness—no birthday cake.
What can I do?

The pot is by the fire.
The water in the pot is hot.
If I put something in the water,
I can make Birthday Soup.
All my friends like soup.

Let me see what we have.
We have carrots and potatoes,
peas and tomatoes;
I can make soup with
carrots, potatoes, peas and tomatoes."

So Little Bear begins to make soup
in the big black pot.
First, Hen comes in.
"Happy Birthday, Little Bear," she says.
"Thank you, Hen," says Little Bear.

Hen says, "My! Something smells good here.
Is it in the big black pot?"

"Yes," says Little Bear,
"I am making Birthday Soup.
Will you stay and have some?"

"Oh, yes, thank you," says Hen.
And she sits down to wait.

Next, Duck comes in.

"Happy Birthday, Little Bear," says Duck.

"My, something smells good.

Is it in the big black pot?"

"Thank you, Duck," says Little Bear.

"Yes, I am making Birthday Soup.

Will you stay and have some with us?"

"Thank you, yes, thank you," says Duck.

And she sits down to wait.

Next, Cat comes in.

"Happy Birthday, Little Bear," he says.

"Thank you, Cat," says Little Bear.
"I hope you like Birthday Soup.
I am making Birthday Soup."

Cat says, "Can you really cook?
If you can really make it,
I will eat it."

"Good," says Little Bear.
"The Birthday Soup is hot,
so we must eat it now.
We cannot wait for Mother Bear.
I do not know where she is.

"Now, here is some soup for you, Hen,"

says Little Bear.

"And here is some soup for you, Duck,

“and here is some soup for you, Cat,

and here is some soup for me.

Now we can all have some Birthday Soup.”

Cat sees Mother Bear at the door,

and says, "Wait, Little Bear.

Do not eat yet.

Shut your eyes, and say one, two, three."

Little Bear shuts his eyes
and says, "One, two, three."
Mother Bear comes in with a big cake.
"Now, look," says Cat.

"Oh, Mother Bear," says Little Bear,
"what a big beautiful Birthday Cake!
Birthday Soup is good to eat,
but not as good as Birthday Cake.
I am so happy you did not forget."

"Yes, Happy Birthday, Little Bear!"
says Mother Bear.
"This Birthday Cake is a surprise for you.
I never did forget your birthday,
and I never will."

LITTLE BEAR GOES TO THE MOON

"I have a new space helmet.

I am going to the moon," said Little Bear to Mother Bear.

"How?" asked Mother Bear.

"I'm going to fly to the moon,"

said Little Bear.

"Fly!" said Mother Bear.

"You can't fly."

"Birds fly," said Little Bear.

"Oh, yes," said Mother Bear.

"Birds fly, but they don't fly to the moon.

And you are not a bird."

"Maybe some birds fly to the moon,

I don't know.

And maybe I can fly like a bird,"

said Little Bear.

"And maybe," said Mother Bear,
"you are a little fat bear cub
with no wings and no feathers.

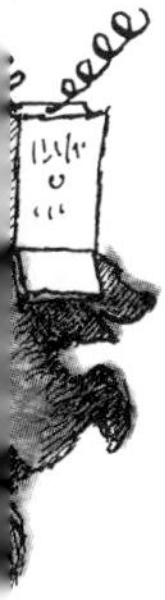

"Maybe if you jump up
you will come down very fast,
with a big plop."

"Maybe," said Little Bear.
"But I'm going now.
Just look for me up in the sky."
"Be back for lunch," said Mother.

Little Bear thought.

I will jump from a good high spot,

far up into the sky,

and fly up, up, up.

I will be going too fast

to look at things,

so I will shut my eyes.

Little Bear climbed to the top of a little hill,

and climbed to the top of a little tree,

a very little tree on the little hill,

and shut his eyes and jumped.

Down, down he came with a big plop,

and down the hill he tumbled.

Then he sat up and looked around.

"My, my," he said.

"Here I am on the moon.

“The moon looks just like the earth.

Well, well,” said Little Bear.

“The trees here look just like our trees.

The birds look just like our birds.

"And look at this," he said.

"Here is a house that looks just like my house

I'll go in and see what kind of bears live here.

"Look at that," said Little Bear.

"Something to eat is on the table.

It looks like a good lunch for a little bear."

Mother Bear came in and said,

"But who is this?

Are you a bear from Earth?"

"Oh, yes, I am," said Little Bear.

"I climbed a little hill,

and jumped from a little tree,

and flew here, just like the birds."

Well," said Mother Bear.

My little bear did the same thing.

Ie put on his space helmet and flew to Earth.

o I guess you can have his lunch."

Little Bear put his arms around Mother Bea

He said, "Mother Bear, stop fooling.

You are my Mother Bear

and I am your Little Bear,

and we are on Earth, and you know it.

Now may I eat my lunch?"

"Yes," said Mother Bear,

"and then you will have your nap.

For you are my little bear,

and I know it."

LITTLE BEAR'S WISH

"Little Bear," said Mother Bear.

"Yes, Mother," said Little Bear.

"You are not asleep," said Mother Bear.

"No, Mother," said Little Bear.

"I can't sleep."

"Why not?" said Mother Bear.

"I'm wishing," said Little Bear.

"What are you wishing for?"

said Mother Bear.

"I wish that I could sit on a cloud
and fly all around," said Little Bear.
"You can't have that wish, my Little Bear,"
said Mother Bear.

Then I wish that I could find a Viking boat,"

aid Little Bear.

And the Vikings would say,

Come along, come along!

Here we go. Away! Away!' "

You can't have that wish, my Little Bear,"

id Mother Bear.

"Then I wish I could find a tunnel,"
said Little Bear.
"Going all the way to China.
I would go to China and come back
with chopsticks for you."
"You can't have that wish, my Little Bear,"
said Mother Bear.

"Then I wish I had a big red car,"

said Little Bear.

"I would go fast, fast.

I would come to a big castle.

"A princess would come out and say,
'Have some cake, Little Bear,'
and I would have some."
"You can't have that wish, my Little Bear,"
said Mother Bear.

"Then I wish," said Little Bear,
"a Mother Bear
would come to me and say,
'Would you like to hear a story?' "
"Well," said Mother Bear,
"maybe you can have that wish.
That is just a little wish."
"Thank you, Mother," said Little Bear.
"That was what I really wanted
all the time."
"What kind of story would you
like to hear?" said Mother Bear.
"Tell me about me,"
said Little Bear.
"Tell me about things
I once did."

"Well," said Mother Bear,

"once you played in the snow,

and you wanted something to put on."

"Oh, yes, that was fun,"

said Little Bear.

"Tell me something more about me."

"Well," said Mother Bear,

"once you put on your space helmet

and played going to the moon."

"That was fun, too,"

said Little Bear.

"Tell me more about me."

"Well," said Mother Bear,

"once you thought you had no Birthday Cake,

so you made Birthday Soup."

"Oh, that was fun," said Little Bear.

"And then you came with the cake.

You always make me happy."

"And now," said Mother Bear,

"you can make me happy, too."

"How?" said Little Bear.

"You can go to sleep,"

said Mother Bear.

"Well, then, I will," said Little Bear.

"Good night, Mother dear."

"Good night, Little Bear.

Sleep well."

The End

Little Bear's Friend

LITTLE BEAR'S FRIEND

An I CAN READ Book®

by ELSE HOLMELUND MINARIK

pictures by MAURICE SENDAK

by the author and artist of LITTLE BEAR

HarperTrophy®
A Division of HarperCollins*Publishers*

To

Mother and Father

CONTENTS

LITTLE BEAR AND EMILY

Little Bear sat in the top
of a high tree.
He looked all about him
at the wide, wide world.

He saw the green hills.
He saw the river.
And far, far away
he saw the blue sea.

He saw the tops of trees.

He saw his own house.

He saw Mother Bear.

He could hear the wind sing.

And he could feel the wind

on his fur, on his eyes,

on his little black nose.

He shut his eyes,

and let the wind brush him.

He opened his eyes,

and saw two little squirrels.

"Play with us," they said.

"No time," said Little Bear.

"I have to go home for lunch."

He began to climb down,

and saw four little birds.

"Look at us," they said,

"we can fly."

"I can, too," said Little Bear,

"but I always fly down.

I can't fly up

or sideways."

He climbed down some more,
and saw a little green worm.
"Hello," said the little green worm.
"Talk to me."

"Some other time," said Little Bear.
"I have to go home for lunch."

He climbed all the way down,

and there he saw a little girl.

"I think I am lost,"
said the little girl.
"Could you see the river
from the treetop?"

"Oh, yes," said Little Bear,

"I could see the river.

Do you live there?"

“Yes,” said the little girl.
“My name is Emily.
And this is my doll Lucy.”

"I am Little Bear, and
I can take you to the river.
What is in that basket?"

"Cookies," said Emily. "Have some."

"Thank you. I love cookies."

"So do I," said Emily.

They walked along eating cookies
and talking,
and soon they came to the river.

"I see our tent," said Emily,
"and my mother and father."

“And I hear my mother calling,”
said Little Bear.
“I have to go home for lunch.
Good-by, Emily.”

"Good-by, Little Bear.

Come back and play with me."

"I will," said Little Bear.

Little Bear went skipping home.
He hugged Mother Bear and said,
"Do you know what I just did?"

"What did you just do, Little Bear?"

"I climbed to a treetop,
and I saw the wide world.
I climbed down again, and I saw
two squirrels, four little birds
and a little green worm.
Then I climbed all the way down,
and what do you think I saw?"

"What did you see?"

"I saw a little girl named Emily.
She was lost, so I helped her
to get home.
And now I have a new friend.
Who do you think it is?"

"The little green worm,"
said Mother Bear.

Little Bear laughed.

"No," he said, "it is Emily.
Emily and I are friends."

DUCK, BABY SITTER

Owl was having a party.

Little Bear, Emily and Lucy

were on the way to Owl's house.

They came to the pond
where Duck lived.
And there was Duck,
baby sitting.

Little Bear looked at
all the ducklings.

He asked,
"Will the mother duck
be back soon?"

"Oh, yes," said Duck.
"Wait for me.
I can go to the party
as soon as she comes back."

Emily put Lucy down, and said,

"Oh, what darling ducklings.

I wish I could hold one."

"Just call them," said Little Bear.

"My goodness!" said Duck.
"I think I have lost one!"

Little Bear and Emily
began to look for it.

Little Bear looked at
the tall reeds.
He said,
"If I were a duckling,
that is where I would swim.
It would be like swimming
in a forest."

He looked in the tall reeds.

And there was the duckling,
swimming about,
having fun.

"Hello, Little Peep,
I see you,"
said Little Bear.

"Peep!" said the duckling,
and swam out to the others.

Just in time, too,
because his mother had come back.

"Hooray!" said Duck.
"Now I am free.
Now we can go to the party."

They went skipping along.

Emily said,

"I think ducklings are lovely."

"Yes," said Little Bear,

"and owlets are nice, too.

Owl says they are."

Emily laughed.

"Oh," she said,

"I love all little animals."

“Me too,” said Little Bear.

THE PARTY AT OWL'S HOUSE

Little Bear, Emily, Lucy,
Cat, Duck and Hen
all came to Owl's party.

Cat looked at Lucy.

"Who is that?" he said.

"That is Lucy," said Little Bear.

"Lucy is Emily's doll."

"Yes," said Emily.

"And she tells me things.

She wants to tell me something now."

"What?" said Cat.

"I can't hear her."

Emily put her head down

to Lucy's head.

"What is she saying?" asked Hen.

"Yes, tell us," said Duck.

"She is saying," said Emily,
"that she wants to sit up here."
And Emily made Lucy sit
in a little tree.

"See?" said Little Bear.
"Emily knows what Lucy wants."

"Let's eat," said Cat.

Owl came out of his house.

He said,

"Here are the party hats.

Put them on."

So they all put on party hats
and laughed at each other.
Then they sat down to eat.

"Look at Lucy!" said Duck.
"She wants to come down!"

They all looked, and there was Lucy, coming down all by herself.

"Oh—Oh!" cried Emily.
"Lucy will break."

And Lucy did break.
She broke her arm.

“Oh, Lucy!”

Emily was crying.

She picked up her doll,

and hugged her.

“Don’t cry, Emily,” said Little Bear,

“we can fix her.”

"I'll get some tape," said Owl.

So Little Bear fixed Lucy.

"There," he said.
"Ask her how she feels now."

Emily put her head down to Lucy.

"She says she feels fine,"
said Emily.
"And she says you are
a very good doctor, Little Bear."

"Tell her thank you,"
said Little Bear.
"Any time she breaks an arm,
or a leg, I will fix it."

Owl laughed.
"No more today, please,"
he said.

Emily made Lucy sit down.

Hen asked,
"Is she saying something?"

"Yes," said Emily,
"she wants us to begin the party."
And that is just what they did.
It was a very fine party, indeed,
even for Lucy.

She said so herself.

"YOUR FRIEND, LITTLE BEAR"

Summer was over,

and Emily was saying good-by.

It was time to go

back to school.

Mother Bear baked a cake.
Little Bear made lemonade.

Mother Bear said,
"Let us eat up all the cake.
If we do, then it will not
rain tomorrow."

"Let it rain," said Little Bear.
"Emily will not be here tomorrow
to play with me."

"Anyhow," said Emily,
"we can eat up the cake.
And we can drink the lemonade."

So they ate the cake,

and drank the lemonade,

and talked and talked.

Then it was time

for Emily to go home.

Father Bear said,

"Don't let Lucy break

any more arms."

"Oh, no," said Emily.

Emily hugged her doll, and said,
"Lucy wants to say good-by, too.
Say good-by to Little Bear, Lucy."

Emily made Little Bear hold Lucy.

Then she said to him,

"Little Bear, you can have Lucy for keeps.

I will give her to you."

"Oh—" began Little Bear.

But before he could say anything,
Emily took Lucy back again.

"Oops!" she said. "I forgot.
Lucy has to come to school with me."

Emily opened her pocketbook.

She took out a fine new pen.

"This is for you," she said.

"I want you to have it."

Little Bear took the pen.

"Thank you, Emily," he said.

He ran into his room,

and came back with a pretty toy boat.

"This is for you," he said.

"For keeps.

You can sail it in your bathtub."

"Thank you," said Emily. "I will.

Good-by, Little Bear.

See you next summer."

Little Bear stood at the door

till Emily was out of sight.

Two big tears ran down his face.

Mother Bear saw them,

and took him on her lap.

"My goodness, Little Bear," she said.

"You will be going to school, too,

and you will learn to write.

Then you can write to Emily."

"Little Bear can begin right now,"

said Father Bear.

He got out some paper, and said,

"Little Bear can write his own name."

"Yes," said Mother Bear,

"with his fine new pen."

She took Little Bear's paw in hers,

and helped him to begin—

That made Little Bear very happy.

He said,
"When can I write to Emily?"

"Soon," said Mother Bear.

And soon he did write to Emily,

like this:

Dear Emily:

It is snowing.

I love the snow.

I wish I could send you some.

Owl, Duck, Hen and Cat

send their love.

So do the ducklings.

I cannot wait for summer.

Your friend,

Little Bear.

Little Bear's Visit

Books by Else Holmelund Minarik

Pictures by Maurice Sendak

LITTLE BEAR
FATHER BEAR COMES HOME
LITTLE BEAR'S FRIEND
LITTLE BEAR'S VISIT
NO FIGHTING, NO BITING!

LITTLE BEAR'S VISIT

An I CAN READ Book®

by ELSE HOLMELUND MINARIK

pictures by MAURICE SENDAK

HarperTrophy®
A Division of HarperCollins*Publishers*

To all grandparents

and all grandchildren

CONTENTS

GRANDMOTHER AND GRANDFATHER BEAR

One day Little Bear came to visit
Grandmother and Grandfather Bear
in their little house
in the woods.
This was something Little Bear
liked to do.

He liked to look at all

the nice things,

the pictures,

Grandmother's flowers,

Grandfather's toy goblin that

jumped up and down in a jar.

He liked to put on Grandfather's

big hat and say, "Look at me!"

And he liked Grandmother's cooking

very, very much.

He had some bread and jam,

cake and cookies,

milk and honey,

and an apple.

“Have some more,” said Grandmother.

“Yes, thank you,” said Little Bear.

“I am not eating too much, am I?”

"Oh no, no!" said his grandmother.
Then Grandfather said to Little Bear,
"We will have lots of fun today,
you and I."
"Yes," said Little Bear.
"But Father Bear told me
not to make you tired."
"Me—tired?" said Grandfather.
"How can you make me tired?
I am never tired!"
He got up and did a little jig.
"Never tired!" he said,
and sat down.

Little Bear laughed

and clapped his paws.

"Do you know what?" he said

to his grandmother and grandfather.

“What?” they asked.

“I like it here,” said Little Bear.

He hugged them.

Little Bear and Grandfather
had all the fun they could think of.
Then Grandfather Bear sat down.
"Now we can have a story,"
said Little Bear.

“Good,” said Grandfather Bear.

“Tell me a story.”

“No!” Little Bear laughed.

“You tell me one.”

“Then I must have my pipe,”

said Grandfather.

Little Bear ran into the house,

got the pipe, and ran back.

But there was Grandfather,

fast asleep!

“Aw—” said Little Bear.

He was sad, but not for long.

He went looking for his grandmother,

and found her in the garden.

Could Grandmother tell him a story?

Oh yes, she could.

She took Little Bear's paw.

"Let us go to the summer house,"

she said. "It is cool there.

Come, Little Bear, let's skip!"

"Oh Grandmother." Little Bear laughed.

"How you skip!"

"You skip nicely too,"

said Grandmother.

They sat down in the summer house.

Little Bear said,

"Tell me a story about Mother Bear,

when she was a little cub.

About Mother Bear and the robin.

I like that story."

"Very well," said Grandmother.

And so, she began.

MOTHER BEAR'S ROBIN

One spring day,

when Mother Bear was little,

she found a baby robin in the garden.

A baby robin, too little to fly.

“Oh, how sweet you are,” she said.

“Where did you come from?”

“From my nest,” said the robin.

“And where is your nest, little robin?” asked Mother Bear.

“I think it is up there,” said the robin.

No, that was a bluebird's nest.

"Maybe it is over there,"
said the robin.

No, that was an oriole's nest.

Mother Bear looked all over,
but could not find a robin's nest.

"You can live with me," she said.
"You can be my robin."

She took the robin in the house,

and made a little home for it.

"Please put me by the window,"

said the robin.

"I like to look out at the trees

and the sky."

Mother Bear put it by the window.

"Oh," said the robin,

"it must be fun to fly out there."

"It will be fun to fly in here,

too," said Mother Bear.

The robin ate. It grew. It sang.

Soon it could fly.

It flew about the house.

And that was fun,

just as Mother Bear had said.

But then one day, it was unhappy.

Mother Bear asked,
"Why are you so sad, little robin?"

"I don't know," said the robin.
"My heart is sad."

"Sing a song," said Mother Bear.

"I cannot," said the robin.

"Fly about the house,"
said Mother Bear.

"I cannot," said the robin.

Mother Bear's eyes filled with tears.
She took the robin out
into the garden.

"I love you, little robin," she said.
"But I want you to be happy.
Fly away, if you wish.
You are free."

The robin flew, far up
into the blue sky.

It sang a high, sweet song.

Then down it came again,
right down to Mother Bear.

“Do not be sad,” said the robin.

“I love you, too.

I must fly out into the world,

but I will come back.

Every year I will come back.”

So Mother Bear kissed the robin,
and it flew away.

"And it came back, Grandmother.
Didn't it?"

"Oh yes, Little Bear.
It came back.
And its children came back.
And its children's children—
here is one now."

"Ah—" said Little Bear.

"I would have let the robin

go free, too, Grandmother.

Just as Mother Bear did."

"Hurrah!" cried Little Bear.

"Here is Grandfather."

"Then it is coffee time,"

said Grandmother.

She went into the house.

Grandfather looked at Little Bear.

Little Bear looked at Grandfather.

They both laughed.

"How about a goblin story?"

asked Little Bear.

"Yes, if you will hold my paw,"
said Grandfather.

"I will not be scared,"
said Little Bear.

"No," said Grandfather Bear.
"But I may be scared."

"Oh Grandfather!
Begin the story."

So Grandfather began.

GOBLIN STORY

One day a little goblin

went by an old cave.

It was old,

it was cold,

it was dark.

And something inside it went bump.

What was that?

BUMP!

“Hoo-ooh—” cried the goblin.

He got so scared that he jumped right out of his shoes.
Then he began to run.

Pit - pat - pit - pat - pit - pat—

What was that?

SOMETHING was running after him.

Oh my goodness, what could it be?

The goblin was too scared to look back.

He ran faster than ever.

But so did the SOMETHING that went

pit - pat - pit - pat - pit - pat—

The goblin saw a hole in a tree.

He jumped inside to hide.

The pit - pat - pit - pat came closer,

closer—CLOSER— till it stopped,

right by the hole in the tree!

Then all was quiet.

Nothing happened.

Nothing.

The little goblin wanted to peek out.

It was so quiet.

Should he peek out?

Yes, he would. He WOULD peek out!

And he did.

"Eeeeeh—!" cried the goblin.

Do you know what he saw?

He saw— his SHOES!

His own little shoes

—and nothing more.

"Goodness," said the goblin,

hopping out of the tree.

"That old bump in the cave
made me jump right out of my shoes.
But they came running after me,
didn't they!
And here they are!"

He picked up his shoes,

hugged them,

and put them back on.

"Good little shoes," said the goblin. "You didn't want to stay behind, did you!" He laughed.

"Who cares about an old bump, anyway," he said.
So he snapped his fingers, and skipped away—

"—just like that!" said Grandfather.

"I can't jump out of my shoes," said Little Bear, "because I don't have any."
He chuckled.
"That's how I like it."

NOT TIRED

Little Bear lay on the sofa.

He was waiting for Mother Bear

and Father Bear to come

to take him home.

He said to himself,
"I am not tired.
I can shut my eyes,
but I will not go to sleep.
I am not at all tired."

He shut his eyes.

He heard a door open.
He heard Mother and Father Bear say
hello to Grandmother and Grandfather.
He heard them come to the sofa.

But he did not open his eyes.

"Ah," said Mother Bear.

"He is sleeping.

How sweet he is!"

Father picked up Little Bear and said,
"Yes, he is a fine little cub.
Tomorrow I will take him fishing."

"Look at him," said Grandmother.
"He is such a good little one."

"And clever, too," said Grandfather.

"Just like me."

They laughed.

Little Bear opened his eyes.

He said to Father Bear,

"Will you really take me fishing?"

"You scamp!" said Mother Bear
to Little Bear.
"You were not really asleep.
You heard about going fishing.
You heard all we said about you!
I can see it in your eyes!"

Little Bear chuckled.
He said to his grandfather,
"We had fun, didn't we?
And you are not tired,
are you, Grandfather?"

"Oh, no," said Grandfather Bear.
"A little cub like you,
and a grandfather like me,
we never get tired, do we?
We can sing and dance,
and run and play all day,
and never get tired."

Little Bear smiled.

He was growing sleepier

and sleepier.

Grandfather Bear went on,

"Yes, yes, yes! We can have

many good times, you and I.

But we never, never get tired!

You are not tired,

are you, Little Bear?

"Little Bear,"

said Grandfather,

"—are you tired?"

Little Bear was not tired!

No!

Little Bear was fast asleep.